Unsolved Mysteries

Unsolved Mysteries

Marie Buck

ROOF BOOKS
NEW YORK

ISBN: 978-1-931824-89-7
Library of Congress Control Number: 9781931824897

Cover art and design by Holly Melgard
Back cover photo by Anjali Khosla

Acknowledgments: Poems in this book have previously appeared in
The Brooklyn Rail, *The Build*, *The Detroit Socialist*, *Elderly*, *Paint-bucket*, *A Perfect Vacuum*, *Prelude*, *Proletarian Poetry Party Chicago: The Zine*, and *Shitwonder*. I'm grateful to the editors of those publications.

Many thanks to Josef Kaplan, Aaron Winslow, Joey Yearous-Algozin, and Steven Zultanski, who helped me revise early drafts of this book.

I'm grateful to Leanh Nguyen, who changed my life and my writing practice.

This book is for Lenora Hanson.

 This project is supported, in part, by an award from the National Endowment for the Arts.

 This book is made possible, in part, by the New York State Council on the Arts with the support of Governor Andrew Cuomo and the New York State Legislature.

Roof Books
are published by
Segue Foundation
300 Bowery, New York, NY 10012
seguefoundation.com

Roof Books
are distributed by
Small Press Distribution
1341 Seventh Street
Berkeley, CA. 94710-1403
800-869-7553 or spdbooks.org

Table of Contents

I. Unsolved Mysteries

II. Documentary

III. Desire

I. Unsolved Mysteries

The Dead

All we're going to do after the revolution is document the lives
of the dead, not the dead we already know about, but the dead we
don't know about.

We're going to take Jeff Bezos's money and we're going to document
ourselves and our pets, all our affections, our quotidian habits.

We're going to document street cats that we didn't take in because
we already had pets.

We're going to document, on behalf of our pets, all the toys that our
pets liked and accidentally destroyed.

And maybe socialism will unveil something. Maybe Jeff Bezos's
money will mingle with his blood and create an effect.

Maybe socialism will undo our deadness, so that we might animate
our archives and interact as the things we left behind: me for
instance as a katamari ball of poems, but mostly emails facilitating
the publication of academic articles (i.e., my day job), of bills paid,
of bizarrely intimate texts with people met online, of graduate
school papers about poetry I no longer like, of an embarrassing
and neurotic google history that wonders at various ages about the
health of my bowels, the relative attractiveness of my genitals, the
addictions of family and friends, about how to find memes that
I can no longer find, about how Pasolini was killed, about the
etiquette for sending sympathy notes.

So that is the body that would get picked back up, and it could go
around and find the others—the archives of my friends and lovers
and pets from across time. I would find my childhood dogs, I
would pet them, I would find the goldfish that got trapped at the
top of the fish tank and cooked under the light—and when I had
gotten used to things a bit and was ready I would find my loves, my

loves across time, here in the form of animated g-chats. I'd suck on the shoulders of the g-chats; I'd be really toppy with them. I'd leave them for my friends, and my friends and I would tease each other about our archive bodies, about the things we'd googled, the way our texts fit together to create new versions of our mouths. Let's take Jeff Bezos's money and use it to live forever.

I Start Watching *Unsolved Mysteries*

If you don't know it, it's a TV show from the late 80s and early
90s—and on up into the aughts, apparently, though I haven't seen
those episodes—about various eerie phenomena: unexplained
deaths, paranormal activity, lost loves, hidden treasure, lost heirs,
UFOs, missing persons, etc. The categories, which at one point in
the opening credits are listed across the screen in a style that
makes them look like they're receding into the depths of the
computer, are loose and vary from week to week. If you remember
the show, you probably remember it for the unexplained death
segments, which mostly recount people going about their daily
routines and then disappearing or turning up murdered. It is, often
but not always, a serialized documentary about the violent deaths
of mostly working-class people, often living in rural places, whose
lives would not otherwise be well-documented. And, like with all
of us, their lives and deaths might have been otherwise.

Hot Jock Shot Wad from Wisconsin 11/85
Saturday the 3rd

In 1985, Dexter Stefonek, a seventy-eight-year-old man,
is killed while traveling
from Oregon to Wisconsin.

It's winter. He chooses to save
time by stopping at rest stops to sleep.
"Hot Jock Shot Wad from Wisconsin 11/85 Saturday the 3rd"
is written on the rest stop bathroom wall. A cryptic phrase,
maybe a clue.

Police discover it months
after they discover
Dexter Stefonek's car burning,
just after his body is discovered

at a county dump, his shoes hanging out
of a pile of garbage. His legs, his body
hidden frozen within the pile.

According to the internet
and also to the office
of Orrin Hatch, who was mocked online
for using the phrase publicly
in August 2017,

"shot your wad"
comes from the Civil War era and refers to
shooting a plug of cloth
rather than a bullet
from a musket. I.e., an ineffective shot,
a shot where you fucked up and wasted it.

But we all know
that if you write on a bathroom wall
that somebody has shot their wad,
you're probably referring to cumming.

Maybe to masturbation
rather than to sex,
but the musket is definitely a dick.

There is even more mystery, though.
The dates are wrong.
Dexter Stefonek's car was found
burning on November 19, 1985, not November 3rd.

November 3rd, then, must've marked a parallel, a time-split.

A hot jock from Wisconsin shot his wad
in the bathroom stall. Possibly into the mouth
of another man. Possibly into the hand of
another man. Possibly into their own hand,
wishing for a different hand, a hand
that wasn't theirs and that was therefore
less predictable and that would have
taken away the burden of being in control
of each motion, of getting oneself to cum as
opposed to being made to cum.

Being made to cum is not always
better, but in a bathroom
stall in Montana in the winter I think it is better.

In this scenario
someone refers to himself as "hot jock,"
which seems surprising. Perhaps this was intended
as a seed: suggest on a bathroom
wall that there is sometimes

a hot jock there,
and then perhaps there will be.

Orrin Hatch was mocked
for saying
that other Republicans
had "shot their wad"
with regard to a series
of defeated health care bills.

The health care bills
sought to make health care even shittier,
to make life and
the relationship to
one's body even more difficult,
so that it would be less
and less likely
that one could sadly
or agitatedly
or happily
or thoughtlessly
shoot one's wad
in a restroom stall
and more and more likely
that one would,
like Dexter Stefonek,
be kidnapped
and shot twice
and left
at an icy garbage dump.

In this world,
the world in which we lose
healthcare and other services
even more quickly than we are,

it is definitely more likely your
car will be set on fire,
your foot will be spotted
sticking out from under an old couch,
your body will no longer be animated.

A friend got caught by a cop
writing "Bernie would have won"
in a rest stop bathroom. That is, casting a
spell.

That world would be a different world.

There are many possible worlds,
some better, some worse than that phrase would suggest.

In one world everyone is
sad about the deaths of their loved ones,
but cross-country trips do not exist,
Montana does not exist,
springtime does not exist.

In this world
you don't have to jerk yourself off,
but you're not jerked off by anyone
else either.

You can touch your dick yourself
or you can thrust it into the world,
and the world manifests not as loose air but as
a sloppy wet mouth,
a rectum,
spit-covered labial folds,
a spongey warm pocket,
a small calloused hand.
You thrust into the world,

you the hot jock,
and you shoot your wad.

My current favorite memory to "shoot my wad" to is:
a man pulls out to avoid cumming,
to keep lasting and make a game of it,
but cannot help but cum accidentally,
sitting in front of me
with his legs folded underneath him, thighs
shaking, spurting into a condom
without touching himself or me.
Just a dick, not being touched,
no longer inside of anything, quivering
and filling a condom head.

This man was definitely not
Dexter Stefonek, since Dexter Stefonek
is dead. But this man came into the aether,
suggesting the possibility
of a world in which Dexter
Stefonek would never have died.

The theory of the homunculus—a
sixteenth-century speculation
about how a fetus came to be—
suggested that cum was composed
of tiny men. Tiny little humans.

So in shooting our hot
wads, we're shooting out people.

Little men who might
escape the condom
not to cream on a hand
or in an ass,
but instead to populate

the world,
to fill it
with
tiny helper-elves, helper-elves
who would've, as
Dexter Stefonek shot his wad
in the rest station bathroom,
left the restroom,
stopped the killer,
a man of a least six feet
with a pale complexion
who was later seen pulling
up behind Stefonek's empty car.

The homunculi
might've restrained the killer,
whispering warnings into his ears
and when he did not heed these warnings,
chomped into his flesh
repeatedly until he melted into the snow
and dissolved into the bellies
of the homunculi,
strengthening them for more good
deeds.

In this world Dexter
Stefonek lives another couple years,
shooting wads where he likes,
quivering and cumming,
driving across the isolated
stretch from Oregon to Wisconsin
over and over again.

Jeremy Bright

A child is left by himself to go to the fair for three days. We're in Myrtle Point, Oregon, in 1986. The child disappears and is later reported missing by his mother.

There are theories:

1. Jeremy ran away with the fair.
2. Jeremy attended a party and was served a drink laced with fentanyl by older kids/adults; the fentanyl aggravated a pre-existing heart condition; he died; the older kids/adults who had served him the drink disposed of the body and didn't tell anyone.
3. Jeremy went swimming with a bunch of other kids and some older guys from the neighborhood. One of the older guys took out a gun and made jokes about it being a toy. Then the older guy pretended to use the child as target practice but in fact accidentally shot him. The older guys took the child to a shack in the woods and tried to nurse him back to health over the course of two weeks. But instead Jeremy Bright died alone in this remote shack in the woods.

There are often rough older kids in *Unsolved Mysteries*. It's a type.

There's a fear of people getting into drugs.

On the East Coast and in the Midwest and, in this case, in Oregon, the murders happen in the woods, but elsewhere they happen in the desert.

Dottie Caylor

When I think of the afterlife, I think of the version in *Beetlejuice*.

Where once you die you continue a version of your life, with your beloved partner, stuck in your beautiful beloved house.

If you go outside, there is a sand worm, and the sand worm is very scary; it seems it could actually cause you to die in the sense of ceasing to exist. But you can also slam the door on the sand worm, stay in your house, and be safe and static with your love. Death is cozy, hygge even.

So as long as your domestic world was good, you'll be okay.

If your domestic world happened to be out of whack at the time of your death, though, things would be different.

Many women on *Unsolved Mysteries* have clearly been killed by their husbands. For instance, Dottie Caylor, an agoraphobic woman who rarely left her house. According to her husband, he dropped her off at the BART station and she never came back.

The husband speculates that the reason she has disappeared is to get on his nerves and irritate him.

It is already clear that, despite the presentation of this sequence of events as a "mystery," the husband killed Dottie Caylor. And the husband has so normalized his abuse that he does not even realize it's probably unwise to say on camera that your missing wife has probably gone missing "just to make things harder" for you.

This woman's life must have been hell.

I want her to have escaped on the BART, but it seems unlikely she was ever headed to the BART. She was, I assume, killed and therefore trapped in her house, like Geena Davis's and Alec Baldwin's characters in *Beetlejuice* are following their car crash, except instead of the house being occupied—or, really, reverse-haunted—by a New York art world family, it's reverse-haunted by her shit husband who killed her, so that she is abused in the afterlife as well as in life.

When I was little, I misinterpreted the ending of *Beetlejuice*. At the credits, we see Winona Ryder asking Geena Davis and Alec Baldwin, who are now her new parental figures, to levitate her since she's done her homework. They do; she levitates and dances in the air to Harry Belafonte's "Jump in the Line (Shake Senora)," meaning that: everyone is happy in the end.

But child-me read the levitating-dancing itself as somehow the point of the movie. I was confused about how climaxes worked in a narrative and was expecting it too late in the film. How could she do that? Was she also dead now? How had she died?

This was part of a larger mistake: as a child I found everything associated with the dead to be frightening and therefore oscillated between correctly reading Davis's and Baldwin's characters as protagonists and incorrectly reading them as terrifying.

The sexiest scene in *Beetlejuice* is the "Banana Boat Song" scene, in which the invading, queer-coded art world family is trying to serve a fancy dinner to potential funders, but is instead foiled by Davis and Baldwin's newfound ability to harness their otherworldly powers. Baldwin and Davis possess them and make their bodies sing and dance to Harry Belafonte's song.

The group dance is erotic; there is an element of otherworldly grotesqueness when their shrimp cocktails become undead hands and grab their faces and then push them away. I could not understand why the characters were dancing—I didn't understand narrative enough to connect it to Barbara's and Adam's actions—and so I was left with the characters' embarrassed faces displaying pleasure and a loss of control at once. It was sex in which the living and the dead are forced to reckon with one another.

The background is minor New York City real estate difficulties, as would be the case for much of my future sex life. Though this would not be the case for Dottie Caylor's life, which took place in the Bay, near the BART, but more precisely within her house, a house I hope she left in death, even if to simply cease, even if her simply ceasing means the rest of us do too.

Kari Lynn Nixon

It's a rainy night in 1987,
and a sixteen-year-old walks
to the store
to get snacks and
vanishes.

Someone checks her
out at the store around 10:05. At around 10:10, a
neighbor walks by her house and doesn't see
her; she goes
missing from about seven hundred feet
from her house.

Did she run away
or was she kidnapped?
Is she still alive?
What was her relationship with her family like,
and does it suggest she would never have run away?

Her relationship with her family was good.
Evidence: she liked to go bowling with them.
She was a cheery kid and
got along with everyone.
She smiled
in many photos.

Annoyed by adherence to small-town
norms as evidence that
she was happy
and therefore didn't
run away
and therefore
must have been murdered,
I root even harder for her to be alive.

I imagine some scenarios
in which
she leaves because she's being abused
or to go be queer in New York City

or to go do drugs in New York City
or to go be with a lover in New York City.

She's too big for this rural town;
she's suffering for its conservatism. In
the scenario I imagine,
she buys her snacks and her friend shows up,
all according to plan. She gets into the car.
They drive to the city.
They live in a squat.
They find loving chosen families and
fuck up and
fall in love with people
and make weird art, catching the tail end of the "downtown
scene," I speculate.

I.e., this could be a story about liberation.

In real life, two years later, Kari Lynn's parents watch
a New Kids on the Block video
and see her face in the crowd.

She's jumping around
dancing. And her parents can see that the girl
in the video, like Kari, has four earrings in her left ear,
which I take to be good evidence that she was
rebellious and looking for a different life,
despite the fact that New Kids on the Block is the opposite
of punk, and I think if you were going to flee upstate New York
for something else, that something else would
probably not be the New Kids on the Block.

Authorities ask the New Kids if they know Kari.
They don't, but they do volunteer to appear on *Unsolved
Mysteries* to plead with Kari to come home. It's Jordan
Knight and Jonathan Knight. Brothers, the two cutest
in the band, who now look so young, as young as
the members of ACT UP in the ACT UP documentaries
I've just watched. The clothes are the
same; the haircuts are the same.
I'm watching *Unsolved Mysteries* lying
chastely on someone else's bed.
We both pet the cat, we brush hands,
we look up which of the New Kids would later turn out to be
queer: Jonathan Knight.

It's 1989. Kari is either dead or going to concerts.
Jonathan and Jordan are on TV
pleading with her to return to her family—
this is thoughtless of them, she must've left because her family
was fucked up, I say. Why tell her to narc on herself?

Elsewhere people
wearing the same clothes as the New
Kids are sitting in at the FDA.

Jordan and Jonathan talk like the people in
ACT UP, like people talked in 1989 rather than now,
rather than in the 70s.
It's 1989 and
I'm sitting in my bedroom,
putting together a heart-shaped jigsaw puzzle of
Jordan Knight's face,
feeling desire
or perhaps
feeling that this person
is an appropriate object for my proto-desire.
Jordan and Jonathan don't yet

look to me like they're from ACT UP;
I haven't seen footage of ACT UP;
ACT UP has not yet been so effective
as to be televised into rural households
with seven-year-olds
who assemble Jordan Knight's face
into a heart shape.

I hope Kari is in New York City,
but instead,
at the end of the episode
we get a perfunctory update:
Kari was raped and murdered by a neighbor
who buried her body in his parents' yard.
Kari never went to a New Kids concert; she
never escaped upstate New York;
the girl at the concert was some
other girl who looked like her, who
could be alive or dead right now,

who probably knows she's in the video
for that New Kids concert,
who might know she looked, as a child,
like Kari Lynn Nixon,
but who definitely doesn't know
I'm writing this poem.

Dream in Which You Are Ineffectively Surveilled

At a political meeting, I am told by someone who would know that you should assume the government is reading everything you write and hearing everything you say.

If you're putting it on a screen—in Word, in text, wherever—they're collecting it. We can make it harder for them with things like Signal, but the only real obstacle they have to knowing everything you write and say is that there is too much data.

That is, the technology to actually sift through all these sounds and words isn't there yet, though they're working on it.

And so you should assume everything on a screen is being read. And everything you say is being heard.

I.e., the abundance of our writing and talking is what interferes with the government's ability to surveil us. The more we write and talk the better.

Your phone is listening in therapy, for instance.

It's reading the sadnesses you convey to friends via text or email or on a walk back from the gym or huddled up in a bar corner.

It knows all your complaints and desires.

And since it's not selective in what it listens to, in hearing the voices of our comrades at meetings discussing communication platforms and arguing about approaches to protesting ICE, it also hears our desire for love.

Joke's on them; capitalism makes people too lonely to surveil.

If we all text each other enough, surveillance will fail; the nurture that our phone notifications provide will cast a spell to create more time.

We'd all lie around in a giant king-sized bed, fucking in various configurations until someone, getting slightly soft, tried to figure out what was wrong and get back into it, snuck off to the kitchen for water while everyone else continued, tripped over the cat dish and spilled cat food on the floor, etc., then checked their phone and saw something awful was happening.

And once everyone had exhausted themselves, our genitals would change back to crotches, to Barbie-doll-style, non-needy plastic hinges, allowing us to think more clearly.

Desire satisfied, we'd begin to experience more desire, but—since we knew the political situation—we could channel that desire, brushing our lips over one another's plastic, smoothed-over labia and clits until the brushing produced something that was not cum, and also not a weapon, but instead a device, a device that embedded us more concretely into ourselves and expanded the time that we would have: we would go to the meeting, we would print the fliers, we would show up to the demos, we would attach ourselves to others, all without losing our jobs, without petting our cats any less frequently, without losing the moment in which we, drifting to sleep, shoot back up having dreamt ourselves stepping off a surface into nothing; even that dumb moment that we hate even in the moment itself, feeling our pulses surge with anxiety, even that moment would stay with us as long as we wanted it to.

We would do this nightly: we would return home, we would fuck again, we would fall asleep on one another on a couch, we would make food, we would lie in each other's arms, we would talk, we would feel our desire surge, we would fuck, we would come home from work and work more, we would have a capacity for stressful project management tasks, we would fuck some more, our genitals would oscillate from the form for sexual desire to the form for political desire and back again, over and over, getting wet and not wet, flooding each other's chins and then retracting into little hills, we'd watch a labor documentary together, we'd eat something, we'd fall asleep, our bodies still untaxed by days of endless work.

And so knowing this is possible, we produce text that is only about love, no one cares to read it, rudimentary AI skims our sexts, here we are doing push-ups, but here we're thinking about you cumming on our faces, here is an animal, here is some funny garbage on the street, what are you doing later, here look at us and we'll look at you, I put lube on my fingers, I rub my face in an armpit. There are so many of us here, but, as though we're dreaming, the scene shifts suddenly.

Let's Memorialize the Dead Even More

Leftists die and people post "so-and-so, presente" on FaceBook.

The internet right at this moment tells me that *presente* means that the person is present. "You are here with us, you are not forgotten, we continue the struggle in your name."

This is the opposite of what I had imagined it to mean. Not knowing Spanish and not looking it up for years, I had imagined it to mean something more like "I present this person to you," and I can present them because they're dead and therefore finished.

The real version is much better but also sadder.

I watch *United in Anger*, a documentary about ACT UP, and in it beautiful people in their cute 80s clothes go to the AIDS quilt demonstration for World AIDS Day and then stage a separate protest, the protest that David Wojnarowicz suggests in *Close to the Knives*: they throw their lovers' ashes onto the White House lawn. In *How to Survive a Plague*, the other ACT UP documentary, you just see little bursts of ashes-cloud as people throw their lovers' ashes over the fence. But in *United in Anger*, you see a slightly different set of footage. Here you see people open the vessels they are using to carry the ashes and show the contents to the camera.

And the ashes seem thicker, there are maybe bits of bone? Remains look more like remains when they are in vessels than they do when they are clouds dissipating into the air.

It feels like the time I watched Stan Brakhage's autopsy movie, *The Act of Seeing with One's Own Eyes*, curled up on a couch with friends, and I saw the scalp pulled back to reveal that the brain is green, and I could not forget it.

I find it reassuring to think that the ashes aren't really the only remainder: there must be many pictures, maybe some video. The ashes in the boxes look like the lung that is crushed in a doctor's hand in the documentary *Harlan County, USA*. *Harlan County, USA* documents a miners' strike in the early 70s. In the segment on black lung, a doctor or perhaps a union man holds something black and small and crumbly; it looks like paper in his hand, and, closing his hand, he lets it crumble and disintegrate into something even more like old brittle paper; the bits of lung fall through his fingers to the floor.

Later in the movie, a woman stands before a crowd at a solidarity demo for the miners, and, while she's not a miner, she's as close to a miner as you could get, she says, through her son, her father, her husband having been miners. She was there in the 30s for Bloody Harlan County. She tells the crowd they have nothing to lose but their chains. She sings the song she wrote back in the 30s, "Which Side Are You On?"

I.e., this woman is the woman who wrote "Which Side Are You On?"

Harlan County is an observational documentary that insists on giving you no context for anything, so I look her up. Her name was Florence Reece. Her husband was Sam Reece. They were strike leaders and their home was broken into and they were terrorized by the mining company and the law. I have never heard her or his name before, despite that I once wrote a dissertation that was largely about the history of social movements.

A lover tells me about reading *Anna Karenina*. "Are you reading it because Tolstoy was an anarchist?" I ask. "I mean, that's related," he says, "but I just don't want to not have read it." I tell him that's how I feel about *Moby Dick*.

If I don't read it, it will never have entered my brain and I'll die without having read it. My brain will go green without *Moby Dick* or *Anna Karenina* in it.

Though unless you have an autopsy, maybe your brain won't even have the chance to be exposed to air and become green instead of pink. What color is it when dead but not exposed to air? I'm going to assume gray. Your gray brain would never have registered *Anna Karenina* or *Moby Dick*, and it would not matter at all. The brain winds up gray either way, and in that state cannot articulate what it once thought of *Moby Dick* or *Anna Karenina*. It is very unlikely anyone will ever even wonder if you read *Anna Karenina*.

My lover, who is not available to me and with whom I am not in love, tells me about the plot. The plot mostly seems to involve people falling in love with people who are not available to them and being overwhelmed by sadness.

For reasons that are unclear to me, my conversations with this lover tend to circle back to work, exes, and prior sex we've had. His ex, he reveals, makes labor documentaries.

I like that the lung in *Harlan County* and the ashes in *United in Anger* live on in the documentaries, and I wonder what it would mean if they had lived on in the footage, but the documentaries had never been completed, and the footage had sat in a box in a room for many years until it too began to deteriorate, much like the lung.

So that, say, the lung was lost to history except for its documentation on a strip of film, and then that strip of film also crumbled like a lung—but this crumbling of the film strip was itself recorded, so that instead of watching footage of a lung crumbling in someone's hand we would watch footage of footage of a lung crumbling in someone's hand, itself being crumbled in someone's hand.

Sex fluids stain the comforter and look like dried salt; blood dries on a condom in a little silver trash can.

And now my pink brain creates fantasies as I rest.

In the fantasies I read a book called *Moby Dick*. When I wake I want to write down the new *Moby Dick*; in the new *Moby Dick* someone is dying of black lung while I'm protesting outside, not dying of anything.

Inside, people are very cold, while outside I too am cold but not nearly as cold. Diana is there and crying a bit; I make a video to capture the sound of the protest; this does not document anything and the hardware that creates the internet will rot the way that people are left to rot. I will only call it "rotting" if it could be made better, but isn't.

In the dream I go home and am fucked by someone who does not discursively describe the fucking as it's happening, as the other lover, the one who's reading *Anna Karenina*, tends to do.

It is unclear if dirty talk is a kind of documenting—there is no document produced—but saying that you're fucking someone as you're fucking them, and verbally chronicling wetness, heat, rigidity, the swelling of a clit, seems better than to not.

And so in this dream you arrive back from the protest, you're being fucked and only the cumming is verbally chronicled, the rest of it is dissolves more quickly than speech; in the dream your brain turns gray, but in real life it is full of blood.

Should Your Sexuality Be Circuited Through the Ways That Animals Sleep?

I watch the documentary *God's Country*. Everybody from Minnesota in 1985 is hot, especially the former high school wrestler who is both a banker and a farmer.

Taking care of the pigs is part of it; taking care of the cows is most of it, he says.

The interviewer asks if he will get a degree in farming.

He answers, you get a degree in pigs every day.

It's not a bad occupation.

The pigs are shown rooting around.

We see the pigs transported and then strung up and dead; we see conveyor belts, and now the pigs are chopped down and made into meat.

A young farmer talks about being his own boss.

It makes you feel good when the crops look good, he says.

Lauren poses a question: what do you dream about when you have sexy dreams?

But I don't have sexy dreams, or rather my dreams are exactly as sexy as the real situation. I sleep luxuriously alone, or I sleep with a lover and tell myself it's nice to sleep on top of one another, like animals do. And it is: I sleep dreaming of my lover's presence, meaning that I'm dreaming real life.

4/20

Tomorrow is Hitler's birthday.
Tomorrow is the birthday of
an ex of mine's grandmother.
She would never celebrate her
birthday on her birthday, because
Hitler's birthday was, as she said,
nothing to celebrate. We'd go to the
retirement home on a day that was not
her birthday and eat eggs; the food
was very good in the restaurant
section of the fancy retirement
home. Later she would die there
in a place that made good eggs and
that had a lovely balcony area where
people would sit and visit their
relatives, remembering and also not
remembering the details of their lives.

Once I drove from Charleston, where
I went to school, back home to my smaller,
shittier hometown, listening to the Talking
Heads very loudly, and whenever I talk
to someone also from the South about
missing the humidity, this is the moment
I think of,

though now I realize that this is just what I said
then. I was about to leave the South. Alyson,
also about to leave, said she'd miss
the humidity. I drove four hours in AC
listening to the Talking Heads and
now that is the moment I think of
when I think of humidity

despite that it was not humid.

False confidence,
when you imagine
you're leaving your trauma behind.

This is, apparently, a poem about reverie
a poem that takes the form of reverie,
as poems have long done. I used to think
I didn't like reverie. But perhaps I was

wrong. Garfield thinks he hates
Mondays, but really he hates
capitalism, as the internet points out.
As the internet points out, Garfield
thinks he
hates Mondays, but Garfield doesn't
even work. Jon works. Garfield
hates it when Jon goes to work because
Garfield loves Jon.

So, like Garfield, it turns out I love Jon.
Or I love Jon, by which I mean I love the
mundane and clueless presence in my
life. Jon as all my attachments, Jon just
hanging there thick in the air, Jon as the food-
steam I release from my Instant Pot,

sticking to the walls.

The internet has a video of
a cicada yelling "awww yeah."

Also recently I watched a video that
shows a corgi sneaking out to a
fence in the cover of night and

jumping on the back of a small
pony. Then the pony trots
around, with the corgi riding happily.

The people filming and
uploading this scene claim that   .
this is what happens when they're not
looking, which I hope is true. Perhaps

the corgi and the pony were born on
Hitler's birthday. Though it's unlikely,
perhaps they also know this, that they were
born on Hitler's birthday. The pony gives
the corgi a ride and they talk about it
every day. Otherwise the corgi and the
pony are not personified. They don't
understand human things otherwise; they
were just born knowing that the date
was 4/20, that Hitler too was born on
4/20, that Hitler was a fascist
leader who killed unfathomable
numbers of people. They want to talk
about something else as the pony trots
around the yard, as the corgi holds on,
bobbing,
but they have no other thoughts in their little
animal brains and so they don't. The screen
of my phone sweats; I picture a cartoon version
of planet Earth but covered in hair. It's time
to dream.

Unsolved Mysteries

Instead of watching *Unsolved Mysteries*,
I go to an experimental music show at a church,

where I read a text from my mother,
whose hand is dangerously swollen and whose cat
has gone missing.

I sit in the back. I look at
the bench, I want to

lay on the bench, but instead I look up at stained glass
and the eyes of the figures there; I pray for the cat.

Earlier this week I fucked someone with a silicone dick while
someone else fucked me with a real dick and, looking in the mirror,

I could not help but think of Frank

O'Hara's manifesto "Personism," in which O'Hara describes
his new philosophy, Personism, as putting the poem

"squarely between the poet and the person, Lucky Pierre
style" so that "the poem is correspondingly gratified,"

and, many years ago now, an undergrad poetry professor
explaining "Lucky Pierre" to me and my classmates: i.e., the
Lucky Pierre is the man in the middle of a threesome of men,

and the poem is like the man in the middle, the conduit between
the writer and the reader,

and so now I could verbalize this current scenario—verbalize it
in my brain—only as a "Lucky Pierre" scenario

wherein I was a poem, a conduit,
which is also what
it feels like if someone is fucking you from behind

while you lick the clit of someone lying in front of
you, so that each thrust pushes your whole body
and moves your fingers deeper into the body
of your lover; i.e., you're the relay point in any case.

Your experience of the Lucky Pierre
is itself mediated by this 60s gay male term for it;

you can't get to the fucking without going through
"Lucky Pierre," without going through poetry, without going
through Frank O'Hara.

So that the term "Lucky Pierre" from the personism manifesto,
then,
is placed in between yourself and
the experience of the Lucky Pierre, the conduit for thinking

about how hot it is be a conduit, so that your physical body
is in the middle, doubly gratified, like the poem is, but mentally,
you're

behind, topping Frank O'Hara's notion of the poem,
which is gratified, while it tops the physical scene,

the scene in which you are topping and are topped
simultaneously. You fuck this amalgam of Frank

O'Hara and the personism manifesto, your fake
dick floating in and out hugged by

text; it is a PDF of the personism manifesto
that you are fucking, and the PDF in turn fucks

a scene, a scene displayed in a mirror in which your

body leans down over your lover while your other lover,
behind you, catches your eye in the mirror as he thrusts into you;

the mirror is glass but the dick of the PDF is swallowed by
the padded, mysterious feeling of an interior. The stained-

glass window in the church with the experimental
music show isn't fucking anything. Your prayer for
your mother's cat is
working; the cat will return the next

morning. This church bench has a cushion, where sometimes
church benches do not; for religious experiences at church

you are supposed to be uncomfortable, whereas
for chill experiences with ambient music

you are usually supposed to be comfortable, your body
naturally being the conduit between you and the music

so that this current multi-channel piece you are hearing
comes from different parts of the church, some notes

behind you, some in front, some on various sides, making
your body feel like it's in space, which is odd in that it

is obviously already in space, and would be in space
even if the piece were not "multi-channel," but it *is*

multi-channel and you find yourself simultaneously
in a room and

pretending to be in a room,
playing with your necklace,

aware of the body beside you,
a body you'll later penetrate

and which will penetrate you,
though

not simultaneously. There is no
metaphor here.

You could rub against one another
and read a PDF after.

That Optical Illusion Where You Think Someone Else's Arm Is Your Own, Except Instead the Topic Is the Future

It's 2019 and I'm worried an image of my brain is floating above my actual brain. My face is buried between my lover's thighs, and when I lift my head up to concentrate on fingering my lover instead, snot drips down to the space above my lip, a little proclamation but without any content. It's like the snot is asking if it's taking up too much space right now, and the image of my brain, which I have no control over, is reassuring it it's not.

I bury my face in my lover, but that means the crown of my head is turned toward the sun, or rather toward the overhead lighting I had meant to turn off. My eyes shift back in my head, like in the meme, and reveal hammers and sickles in the whites of my eyes, which my lover stares at with excitement, clasping at my shoulders.

I'm picturing the world not being garbage, me and my lover in the non-garbage world feeling not like garbage, grinding our clits against one another's knees and thighs and worrying about nothing, simply coming up with questions: can I put my hand in you, can I put my hand in your mouth, how many ladybugs are moving through the air around us, which tomato vine smells the strongest, can you fashion a dildo from just anything, let's make one that's garden-themed.

A Stream of Discharge Arcs Away from a Nipple

At Greenwood Cemetery, someone named
"Texter" is interred. You can put a picture of
this online and people will like it.

At the cemetery I know ridiculous
Catholic shit, like that
the petals on the flowers of a dogwood tree
correspond to Christ's wounds, one through each foot,
one through each wrist. The person I'm there
with knows ridiculous Mormon shit instead and
starts to tell me it.

As a kid I remember thinking
that it was weird that they put
nails through Christ's wrists rather
than his hands, until someone told me
that if they had put the nails in his
hands, his hands would've just ripped
down the middle. I'm not sure if that's true,
either.

I have, I am finding,
many false
ideas about New York
City Civil War battles
and Civil War veterans,
which my date tolerates while I
fail to show him bright green parrots.

Later I get caught in the rain and feel exhilarated about it.

Later I go to a lover; it is best to sleep in a pile and we do.

Apparently there are 500,000 people
buried in Greenwood Cemetery,
and the pauper's graves were dug
up to make the Gowanus Canal,
so that the rich are still in one pile,
the Greenwood Cemetery pile, and
we the living are all mingling with the other dead; we're
all sleeping in a pile with the non-rich.

The dead version of me dreams of my lover's sister, who I've never
met, handing him her baby, which doesn't exist. She can't take
care of this baby and so my lover takes it.

And,

like in medieval art, the baby looks like a small adult, like a little
mini-version of my lover,
long hair and all,

and my date earlier had worn an earring of two
jumping dolphins in one
ear, and the dolphins now hang
from the lip of this baby, who
has never lived, and who
overlays me and my lover,
as me and my lover lay
alive and warm to each other,
sweating into each other's bodies and then also
the dead among us there
unmoored by the Gowanus Canal and
wandering Dean Street, floating
up to the fourth floor to look at us
through the window, to look at our
faces, which must seem very loud
to them as we cum and as we sleep.

My lover and his new son
are whispering: they get us to turn *Buffy
the Vampire Slayer* back on again. This
is a lot of ghosts; despite the episode
where Buffy uses hammer and sickle-
shaped weapons in her slaying—where
the camera zooms back to show
the weapons in profile and we know what
they are—

despite that, Buffy is not political enough to carry
us anywhere, and so the ghosts of
the Gowanus collapse into the black and white tile floor
to register as dust flecks,
and my dream fades into the aether,
and the cats alone at home whine for me:
what if we just go on like this.

II. Documentary

**There Are Not a Lot of Universes
in Which Time Travel Is Possible**

It's winter 2019. Apparently the very old are waiting to die so that they can live to see the Mueller Report.

NPR says: "some elderly, ill critics of the president say they want to try to hang on to see how it all turns out."

For instance, a World War II veteran named Mitchell Tendler began to fade. And, his son recounts, "it just was quiet for a little while and then he just sits up in bed halfway and looks at me and he goes, 'Shit, I'm not going to see the Mueller report, am I?' And that was really the last coherent thing that he said."

Some of these people will, I imagine, live to be disappointed by the Mueller report, and some of them will die without having seen it, disappointed instead by the timing of their deaths.

It is a shame when people die at the wrong time.

Mark Fisher: January 13, 2017, in the wake of Brexit and then Trump's election, several months shy of June 8th, when Jeremy Corbyn will do unexpectedly well in the snap election Theresa May calls, upsetting the conservative majority and also indicating a larger leftward shift.

Mark Fisher, presente.

You watched the British elections with a new lover who told you everything he knew about the UK as you watched and fooled around and ate Seamless and fooled around and watched more. He had planned to sleep over even though you no longer wanted him to because, even as you were rooting for the same thing, there was a gap between you and him; he stayed; you thought about Mark Fisher's death and were relieved when the lover got up in the morning to go to the bathroom and you were alone in your room, hearing him pee through the bathroom wall but nonetheless alone. The elderly who are waiting to hear the Mueller report will be cordoned off when they're dead, but they will not even hear the world through a bathroom wall; they won't know any of it.

Kathryne Lindberg, my teacher in grad school, who spent her life writing about African American literature and communism, jumped off a bridge into the Detroit River on December 13, 2010. Tarek el-Tayeb Mohamed Bouazizi, a Tunisian fruit vendor, set himself on fire on December 17, 2010, four days later, the flame of his body sparking the Arab Spring, after police officers who regularly harassed him confiscated his fruit and the electric scales that he used to weigh it.

Clearly if you spent your life studying communism and knew that in four days someone else's suicide was about to spark a massive political shift, you would not yourself be able to commit suicide. Clearly if you were Mohamed Bouazizi and knew the effect your immolation would have, you would have to do it anyway, knowing you'd never get to see its effects. Which sounds nearly impossible to do.

I wish they could have negotiated a trade: if Kathryne, Mark Fisher, Mohamed Bouazizi had known when to have hope and when to despair and collectively saved a body for the three of them to animate together, swapping in and out of it, watching events unfold, channeling their rage into this anchor-body that could move in the world if it wanted to, or rest, undead, and watch things get better and worse, better and worse, watch suffering and death, watch joy, in patterns that at least are different than those we might've expected, suggesting the possibility of better patterns yet to come.

The one brief period in which I regularly engaged in "suicidal ideation" —i.e., I did not want to kill myself but enjoyed flirting with the idea every day, noting, with titillation, as the train came, how easy it would be to fall in front of it, whereas normally I tried to avoid thinking about exactly that, and whereas later the thought of the train would not cross my mind—in that brief period of suicidal ideation in 2016, my brain played two thoughts over and over again:

—Why are we still doing this? ("This" being getting up, going to work, everything we associate with "life," tbh.)

And then the response:

—If you stopped doing this, you'd literally never find out what happens next.

It's hard to answer why we're all still doing this, but also very easy to answer why you personally are still doing it: to see what everyone else does. The gap between yourself and others—which we might think is a source of isolation—is actually what keeps you wanting to animate your body.

It's 2011 and you are getting fingered in a bed that belongs to neither you nor the person fingering you; you've taken a break from the protest. You moan; they return it; their finger glows, E.T.-style; your clit glows back; the glowing finger and the glowing clit become vine-like and entangled, become animated by something else, pull the two of you back out into the world.

In 2019 relatives keep dying.

And everyone in your family who has died before seventy has not had money, or even a union job, like your father did.

Your mom's cousin, for instance.

You went to visit your mom's cousin's family when you were ten. Your second cousin, a year older than you, had John Conner hair, per *Terminator II*, and you watched *Doug* with him in his room and your prepubescent body felt a sort of proto-lust. Messy room, skateboarder, John Conner hair.

Terminator II is a movie about the future, and a world in which Skynet, a synthetic intelligence system, has gained consciousness and decided to kill all the humans. In this movie you can travel back and forth in time, altering things, an ability unavailable in real life, so that the proto-lust of a ten-year-old for her eleven-year-old second cousin must remain forever encased in a husk.

There is no way to jostle it or repurpose it; there is no way to feed it to the souls of the dying and use it to reanimate them.

The proto-lust walks in the woods with sticks. It sleeps on an air mattress. It goes away. It returns years later and drives around the Beltway with older teens to watch the Robin Williams movie *Jack*, about a child who looks like a grown man, which is a metaphor for nothing, and it sits, much younger, in the back of a car as the car speeds along, and then it arrives home, where the two sets of parents reminisce about their parents, some of whom are dead, and joke about family traumas. The proto-lust is encased; it cannot be penetrated.

Other lust can do things. It's summer 2018. You want to fuck someone who is texting you about cheap popsicles usually bought in bulk for children. Like, come over, we're going to watch documentaries and eat popsicles, you know: the shitty ones. Freeze pops in plastic tubes. You go to a public swimming pool and talk about Mark Fisher, and also about how this pool wouldn't exist except for the New Deal, *public-fucking-pools, they would never make that now*, as teenagers splash around you. Your prospective lover is reading John Reed's *Ten Days That Shook the World*; water is the best feeling; the lover bails on actually fucking afterward, citing a text received about the illness of a family member; your lust then exists in the form of a freeze pop, slushed up in a plastic tube; the slush in the plastic tube merges with the slush in the freeze pop plastic tubes of your youth; you're eating a freeze pop in your neighbor's backyard; your neighbor shows you a secret; she's written the word "fuck" in marker on the bottom of her shoe; this only increases the power of the freeze pop, which you then make larger, which you then suck on as though it's fingers.

It's 2019, you put your fingers into one person as she lays back on the bed while you ride another person as he too lays back; you make your lover cum with one hand, your forearm hurts, you are sweating; when you pull your fingers back out, your fingers are each a freeze pop covered in her fluids; you raise the freeze pop fingers to your mouth to suck the fluids off, but as you do the plastic part of your fingers dissolves so that the flesh of the fingers itself—the colored ice—melts into your mouth and you're left without fingers.

Okay. You lie in this bed letting people stroke your back while the people with the hardest lives die first; their deaths are the shitty kind.

I was wrong here: you don't get to bottle any of your lust, whether you're ten or thirty-six. You return months later to the lover who took you to the pool and texted you about shitty popsicles. It's morning and cold out and you arrive to his sunny apartment and recover from the walk over and excuse yourself to the bathroom to blow your nose and then enter his room, which has bright yellow sheets. You fuck his face. "You look so happy," he says after, and he's not wrong.

Haunted by a Strange Double

I watch *Eyes on the Prize*, the canonical fourteen-part documentary about the Civil Rights Movement, and in the first episode, Ed Nixon, identified as a Montgomery community leader who worked for the NAACP, talks about the activism that he'd already been doing before the boycott. Montgomery was a fairly organized city, which is one of the reasons that they chose to move forward with a big action there. So this person had been doing things for a while. And he says in the doc, "You know, I was doing this so my kids and grandkids could have a better life. I never thought I would see it. Then the boycott happened and—you see when I first started fighting, I was fighting so that the children came behind me wouldn't suffer the same thing I suffered. Then the night of the bus boycott, on December the 5th, I told the people that I'd done been fighting like that for all these years and tonight I change my mind. I said, Hell, I want to enjoy some of this stuff myself."

*

And now I meet someone who grew up in rural Georgia, a few hours away from where I grew up in rural South Carolina, and he tells me about how heavily the military recruited at his high school, giving students signing bonuses so that they could buy Mustangs with the signing bonuses as down payments, never to be able to pay the monthly payments after. Ready to get sent overseas. Which seemed right to me, but not accurate: I wasn't surprised, but I didn't remember it happening.

And then abruptly I say, even before I realize it, I was in high school before 9/11.

I.e., since I was born about six years before this person, we experienced different levels of military recruitment in our rural Southern high schools.

*

I start watching what happens in the back of a Dallas Neiman Marcus, and for years I never finish.

Frederick Wiseman makes documentaries about the mundane workings of institutions, and this one is about the flagship Neiman Marcus store and corporate headquarters in Dallas in 1983. I make popcorn, I get stoned, I watch it, falling asleep thirty minutes in, over and over again, once a month or so, for years.

We distinguish between import bras and domestic bras; you want to get your customer into an import bra. And if your customer cannot appreciate the cost of an import bra, which might run forty or forty-five dollars, this is an opportunity to get your customer into an import bra at a lower price point; this one is twenty-nine dollars.

The business people in *The Store* are very interested in French pastries. There are Christmas decorations, like in *The Price of Salt*. "The reindeer is a no, but a surprise: I do have the angel." Department stores were once different; salesmanship was once different. A lot of effort. In real life, now, Ben Montero, who makes sweet comics, posted one a few weeks ago. An anthropomorphic bird lies in a casket, while his pallbearer bird-friends carry the casket and the sun looks on with a sad face. The speech bubble of the bird in the casket reads "it is what it is." A phrase that older people, and I guess in this case younger people, say when bad things happen and they've already happened; there is no going back, you think, and the dead recede further into the past and the scene shifts again. It's like time is running through mud. "I'm ready to die for this," you hear one man say to another.

Kurt McFall

There is one *Unsolved Mysteries* episode where a youth, Kurt McFall, gets into Dungeons and Dragons and is taken under the wing of an older man.

Or rather, on further investigation: he was in the Society for Creative Anachronism, an international living history group with the aim of studying and recreating mainly medieval European cultures and their histories before the seventeenth century. And he played a lot of Dungeons and Dragons. But then he also got involved with a pagan cult, according to the show.

According to the show, he became obsessed with this pagan cult.

He drove to San Francisco; he spent the night with an older friend. They had dinner and a movie; at 3 a.m., says the friend, he got up and went out. Later his car was found, with his D&D books in it, a suit of metal armor in the trunk, beer bottles that were not his— he didn't drink—in the front. His body was found in the ocean. He'd fallen off a cliff, or been thrown off a cliff, or been disposed of off a cliff.

Unsolved Mysteries wants to blame the older man, and it codes the relationship as possibly queer. It's clear that pagan cult fears are also queer fears.

I want to code the murder as homophobic instead; maybe Kurt was queer-bashed by whoever had the beer bottles.

It is nice to think that the political wins of recent decades might eliminate acts of violence in the future, that we can keep winning and stop bad things from happening, even though I do not know if this is true.

Kurt's dad says he found in Kurt's room a knife made from a deer's hoof, a necklace of stone and feathers, and drawings of witchcraft and violent fantasies.

It's 1984.

In 1998, I stow a book about paganism in my locker for my friend, so that her mother doesn't find it and burn it, like she did her other pagan books.

When we drop this friend off, we have to go inside so her mom can say hi to us, which really means her mom is looking at our eyes to see if we're high.

We're never high; I didn't smoke weed then, but sometimes we had just come from performing pagan rituals.

The pagan books were probably stolen from Books-A-Million, but the D&D books I had were not; those were given to me by a boyfriend who very much wanted me to like D&D.

I would go with him to play; we played with people we'd met at the gaming store at the mall. We'd go to one couple's trailer to play; they were older; they had a baby; we would take over the living room and create fantasies where people made characters and sometimes the characters were sex jokes. Roll a die to see how big this character's dick is. Roll a die to see how much this character can take.

Sometimes we would go to the boyfriend's giant house on the lake; his European mom would make us mac and cheese; we'd take over the basement, a place where I already spent a lot of time making out and playing old video games. My only desire was to live in the world that the lake house suggested; hungry for worldliness, I put up with going to the trailer so that I would also continue to be invited to the lake house, since the Dungeons and Dragons part was the relevant part for my boyfriend and the glimpse of some sort of perceived cosmopolitanism was the relevant part for me.

Part of me hates snobby younger me, but most of me is like "thank god you had the good sense to want something outside of your town."

My boyfriend's family was cavalier in talking about sex; his mom baked brownies called "chocolate orgasms" and brought them around to everyone saying "would you like an orgasm?"

Across town, an old friend who'd drifted away was shooting cocaine and sleeping with his ex-girlfriend's mother. I don't remember if he was eighteen yet, even. Though I didn't register it as rape at the time.

Back on our side of town, my boyfriend's parents fought and tried to force him to sign up for the military, but I was wooed by their nice coffee table and giant, airy windowed spaces and boat and trees.

Sometimes we made our characters do lesbian things, though never gay things. Meanwhile my previous, pre-boyfriend friends were making out with other women at the nearby college.

We made our characters fuck each other, like playing with Barbies but for teenagers.

I wonder about Kurt McFall's D&D characters, who must have once been written on character sheets, who were likely chronicled by the San Francisco police department with other evidence related to Kurt's death.

You could play a campaign as these characters, the dice telling you how it went down.

You could make his characters have queer sex with each other without fear.

You could have them slit the throats of monsters and live in San Francisco.

You could take them on a campaign, where they'd go to my home-town and rescue everyone who didn't want to be there, then we'd all march cross-country, to rescue Kurt McFall, to kill his killers before they could kill him, a magic missile to the temple.

Why is his name Kurt Mc*Fall*, wtf.

Documentation

Most of the people in *Unsolved Mysteries* would not have very well-documented lives, were it not for their horrible deaths.

There are often a lot of family photos, and some video, and some family and friends and neighbors—but how quickly do you pass from memory? And *Unsolved Mysteries* remains in print, so to speak—you can access it; it will be a long time before it is gone, and the websites about it are gone, and all the remains of every person who once watched it are also gone.

Most of the episodes are about people who lived fairly un-noteworthy lives, but became noteworthy at the moments of their deaths by dying in horrible ways. What I mean to say is that, all things being equal, most of us will work and die, our deaths really registering mostly the fact that we kept doing our jobs and did not throw sand in the gears; the flow of global capital continued on our watches. We had feelings; we loved; we were sad; we loved some more; we died, with regionally- and temporally-specific accents that will soon leave the earth. With trite ideas about our families, or not. *Unsolved Mysteries* documents mostly the working classes, and we are otherwise sparsely documented. That is, the price the working classes can pay to be memorialized is a horrific death.

There is a book called *The Art of Memory*, written by Frances Yates and published in 1966. Diana came across it when she was preparing to write a review of something else; apparently all the experimental writers and artists of the 60s read this book and loved it.

I get the book, which describes a lost history of using visuals for extreme memorization, and really, for record-keeping before people had easy access to paper and print. The origin story is that a poet, Simonides of Ceos, was at a banquet performing a poem. He complimented not the host, but someone else in the poem and got into a sort of weird altercation with his host about it. Later someone wants to see him; he leaves the banquet; while he's gone the roof caves in and kills everyone. The bodies are so mangled that they can't be identified. BUT, Simonides remembers where people had been sitting; he is able to identify the bodies.

Later we get instructions on how to use what is described as the "places and images" method to create a memory system for ideas. You are a lawyer and wish to remember the details of a case and to create a system for it. The prosecutor has said that the defendant killed a man by poison, has charged that the motive of the crime was to gain an inheritance, and declared that there are many witnesses and accessories to this act. You need to create an image to help you begin to store this memory, Yates relays. This image is a sort of file folder, in which you'll store more files. Your instruction:

> We shall imagine the man in question as lying ill in bed, if
> we know him personally. If we do not know him, we shall
> yet take someone to be our invalid, but not a man of the
> lowest class, so that he may come to mind at once. And we
> shall place the defendant at the bedside, holding in his
> right hand a cup, in his left, tablets, and on the fourth finger,
> a ram's testicles. In this way we can have in memory the
> man who was poisoned, the witnesses, and the inheritance.

The cup, Yates explains, "would remind of the poisoning, the tablets of the will or the inheritance, and the testicles of the ram through verbal similarity with TESTES—of the witnesses. The sick man is to be like the man himself, or like someone else whom we know (though not one of the anonymous lower classes)."

That is to say: the lower classes are hard to remember. In this scenario they're not considered as a possible object of memory, and, furthermore, we cannot even be used as tools for the reader to remember something else, since the reader, presumably, literally cannot tell them apart. A man of the lower classes cannot come to mind at once.

But at the same time, we are instructed that it is common sense that it is easier to remember things that are "exceptionally base, dishonorable, unusual, great, unbelievable, or ridiculous"; we remember striking scenes from our childhoods more easily; we remember a solar eclipse more than we remember a sunrise or sunset, as those happen every day. So "we ought...to set up images of a kind that can adhere longest in the memory." We can set up images that are exceptional; we can "ornament some of them, as with crowns or purple cloaks" or by disfiguring them, "as by introducing one stained with blood or soiled with mud or smeared with red paint, so that its form is more striking"; we can bloodstain people when we picture them, and then they are memorable.

In the scene you're bloodstained, having just been beaten up.

That is, there is a sort of back door: you can become, at least, a metaphor to allow people to think about other things if you are lower class but smeared with blood. You can be remembered.

Better yet if you are covered in a green tarp and pinned to a railroad,

if your foot sticks out from beneath a couch, frozen, at an icy Montana garbage dump,

if you disappear over a cliff and are found impaled on the rocks below,

if you're later found buried in the neighbor's back yard.

So we should, I think, invert it and force the rest of the world to be a metaphor for the dead of *Unsolved Mysteries*: the world as a series of red stains that can help us think about the thousand or so people, I'm guessing, who appeared on the show.

For instance, if we wanted to remember Dottie Caylor, we could think of Jeff Bezos smeared with blood, lying outside of his patrol car, with the lanyard of his handgun wrapped around his ankles, handcuffs on his left wrist, the name "Robert" written on his hand, his unit's radar cable wrapped around his neck, and a bullet wound to the head. We would picture a wide, open public space, and put this image there. We know nothing about Dottie Caylor's life beyond her shitty husband's account of it, so I supposed we'd be using this image of bloodied Jeff Bezos to remember the shitty account on *Unsolved Mysteries*. But also: Frances Yates is unambitious. If we're going to create little fetishes for memory, I want this one to tell us more: we picture Bezos marked with red, and what it gives us, the memory it provides, is Dottie Caylor's desires, her relationship with her pets, the feeling of her skin when she'd just moisturized it, then again when it was dry and in need of exfoliation. And whatever else she wants to tell us.

Likewise, we might construct a garish, memorable image by which to remember Kurt McFall. We picture Beverly Sackler with one part of a sweater tied around her neck and the other tied to a bar three feet above the ground; when we think of Sackler positioned like this, face strained for want of oxygen, what is returned to us are the intricacies of Kurt McFall's Dungeons and Dragons campaigns—the names of each player-character, their stats, the plot lines he wrote as DM, the jokes he made with his friends when playing.

Or, for instance, we picture the flip-flops, chair, radio, first aid kit, and lunch of Jim Walton of the Walton family sitting on the shore, but no sign of Jim Walton. And when we picture this what is returned to us is Kari Lynn Nixon, the girl who disappeared from her neighborhood, and her crush and the sensation of eating an ice cream, her pencil on the page, and also the scent of her shampoo, grass stains on her jeans, the texture of a burger as she bites it and heat warping the air above the grill, every bit of her life; we can make a 3D printed model of it all as we envision Jim Walton's abrupt vanishing.

And so instead of the proletariat eking our way into the archive, covered in blood, as mnemonic devices for the historical wealthy to remember the trivialities of their lives, we will use garish images of the wealthy men—not men of the lowest classes, so they will "come to mind at once"—to evoke for us our own dead.

So that, for instance, the thought of a death helps us think of the life of another.

My Death

When I was about sixteen or seventeen, I was proximate to an event that did not appear on *Unsolved Mysteries*, but could've. The scene was the same: the rural working-class middle-of-nowhere, full of astonishing violence.

I used to go to an abandoned state park and practice Wiccan rituals with my friends. We would make frequent trips to Books-A-Million to look through the "spiritual" section, buying books that a beautiful and slightly older Wiccan man recommended. He was out of high school and had read a lot and practiced a lot. We would look over the books and buy some and try to do the basic rituals together. A lot of it involved making a pentagram and then sitting together and silently thinking about first your hands and then your whole body washing into the ground. This seems less dumb to me now than it did for the few years right after I had stopped doing it.

I did this while other people were drinking heavily or doing coke or going to church, and it seems as fine as any of those things, and probably best for me, as I wasn't very good at doing those other things.

So I would go to this place with my friends. It was technically an island in a lake. We would cross a bridge, follow our car's head-lights through winding forest roads with scattered lake houses and get to a gate, which was always open. We would drive through the gate to a second gate, always locked such that cars could not get in but people could go around, park our car, and go through. The second gate always felt like a sort of passage, and we sometimes performed rituals in which we would ask the island if we could come in. We'd go down a narrow path to a paved clearing, then do more rituals. Afterward we would go back to the car and maybe sit on the hood and the ground and talk. I almost wrote that we would talk about our lives, but I do not think we would: we talked about rituals and books that we read; all of it was aspirational to being somewhere else.

Sometimes I would go to the state park with just my boyfriend. We would park at the outer gate and have clumsy but nonetheless novel, and therefore thrilling, sex. If we heard a car or saw lights, we would startle out of our clumsy, effortful sex; he would start the car and pull away as quickly as possible. There was no reason for anyone else to be out there either, and we did not want to meet anyone there.

Sometime in this period something happened. We read about it in the paper: at the dock right by where we parked, a car was set on fire with someone inside. Police found the burnt-out car and the body, which they could not identify. They couldn't tell whether the person was living or had already been killed when the car was set on fire, probably the latter. Presumably, this was related to drugs: people started pointing out that we were along a drug corridor— between Atlanta and Charlotte, or other cities further north, on I-85. I have no way of gauging if this was true, but certainly my town was one of the bigger ones on I-85—three Super Walmarts, a mall, hundreds of churches, rather than fields and woods only.

After the discovery of the burnt-out car and the body, 1) we were not supposed to go out there anymore, since our parents thought it was a bad idea, and 2) we eventually did anyway and found that the energy of the island had changed. There was a drought, which we thought also might be contributing to this change. The plants were dying and a person had died there. The island seemed angry; we were suddenly afraid of it; we imagined that we might be possessed by something. We consulted our books and mostly stopped going.

But it was also a weird sort of counter-confirmation. We thought we ought to be afraid of something spiritual, but actually we just needed to be afraid of something much more concrete: stumbling into whatever sort of shady underground shit had prompted the murder and the burning of the car.

Later I'd make a similar error in college: my housemates and I would walk across the street to explore the abandoned Catholic school across from our house; we wanted the titillation of looking for ghosts, but instead we'd find a bunch of needles and people's stuff. No need to be afraid of ghosts, but you should probably be afraid of our grotesque world putting people in dire straits such that there are places you shouldn't really enter.

I thought maybe I would look up the burning of the car with the body in it and find it—it had been in the news a good bit, though this was in the late 90s. What I get when I google, though, is just an assortment of other rural tragedies, in my town and other towns: flames rip through Anderson tow business, Dallas man decapitates self by attaching rope to a fire hydrant, Walmart security guard shoots "shoplifting" mother dead in parking lot, the body of a fifty-eight-year old used car dealer was found.

In looking up this information, I find a podcast called Small Town Murder. "Two comedians look at a small town, what makes it tick, and a murder that took place there. In depth research, horrible tragedy, and the hosts' comedic spin on the whole thing." At least *Unsolved Mysteries* didn't try to be funny.

I tried to explain to a friend something about my town: it is a terrible place for addicts and alcoholics, since these problems are explained only through religion. I.e., this person is doing a lot of coke and clearly harming themselves; it is because he isn't going to church. These are the kinds of narratives that people have. A few months back, my town was in the news because a young woman had gouged her own eyes out in front of a church because she heard voices telling her to sacrifice her eyes in order to get to heaven. She hallucinated that the world was upside down. She was on a lot of meth. Her mother later explained that her daughter had earlier given into temptation and gotten into pot, and that someone had given her pot laced with meth, which then gave her a meth addiction. Doctors suggested the meth she was on was also somehow laced with something worse than meth.

The point is that there is no separation between the perceived moral failing of not going to church and the perceived moral failing of drug addiction, which means there are no narratives or resources for people who don't believe in a sort of particularly toxic breed of Christianity.

If I were going to be a character on *Unsolved Mysteries*, this is how it would have happened. Three found dead at Apple Island, one the person in the car, who really did die, the other two myself and my boyfriend. Three bodies in a car.

After extinguishing the flames, firefighters found the trio's burned bodies in the back of the SUV. They were later identified as [ ], Don Angenent, and Marie Buck.

Police said it appears that all three died from homicidal violence.

The young couple was partially clothed and police found an additional car belonging to Angenent. They believe the couple did not know the perpetrator.

III. Desire

Daniel Ulf Nilsson

I go upstate; I jog through the cemetery and admire the old grave-
stones and how long people have been dead and that no one thinks
of them anymore. The gravestones are doing their jobs, bearing a
trace of these people a hundred and fifty years later. But then I
come across a shiny new one at the top of a hill, Daniel Ulf Nilsson,
who died in 2016, who was born in 1979, so, three years older than
me. I can tell that the grave is newer because it is glossy and has a
sort of tasteful Fibonacci sequence shell on it—but more because
people have left little rocks on top. When did the rocks get there?
Probably within the past few months; I don't imagine they were
there all winter. But also what would knock them off? Who knows
—things move, that's why the older graves look different. But still.
Daniel Ulf Nilsson was a chef who owned a high-end restaurant in
Hudson. I look him up on something called MyDeathSpace and
read that he took his own life by unknown methods on a family
member's farm. I read an account of an acquaintance, who once
saw him in line when they were both buying Powerball tickets
when the jackpot was especially high, and what they'd do if they
won. Daniel Ulf Nilsson's father was a professional hockey star and
played for Winnipeg and then the New York Rangers in the 70s.

Just before Daniel was born.

People who write about food wrote about Daniel, and it sounds
like he was a really good chef. For instance: "There was no need
for dessert, but good food and fellowship and a few sips of wine
have a way of persuading you to linger longer. Thus it was we
sampled, at $8 apiece, the rich, dark chocolate brulée, redefining
the classic custard as I've never before experienced; a pie-inspired
serving of lemon cream over a crustlike cookie and topped with
flaked meringue, and, my favorite, a serving of whipped, sweet-
ened brie with a blueberry-ginger marmalade and more of that
addictive toast."

And later Daniel would compete on a Guy Fieri reality show, cooking, and give one of his ingredients to another contestant who would go on to win. The next morning I eat breakfast and a woman asks to join me at my table, and we talk about her kid and my not having kids and the things she wishes she'd known about having kids, and I go to sleep that night and dream a scene in which I am caring for kids in my old neighborhood and caring for Lenora's niece and caring for random kids I've never seen, and I like it.

I wonder if Daniel Nilsson's dad will be buried with him on this picturesque hill at the town cemetery.

Many people must've eaten food he made, texted about it to friends perhaps, absorbed it into their bodies, shat out its waste, remembered the taste of his food briefly when having something similar later.

Many people must've had his food while chatting with an old friend or fighting with a partner or sitting happily or melancholically alone, feeling fish eggs burst in their mouths.

It is appropriate that we remember people by their birth dates and death dates, so that if someone approaches a cemetery and thinks with wonder about the past, they can be unmoored by suddenly seeing the dates of one of their contemporaries. Daniel Ulf Nilsson, 1979-2016. And looking him up to find him. Making food, getting awards, etc. So that one doesn't feel a sublime sense of the past, but a jarring sense of the present, and not having him there, despite never having known him.

Take My Glasses Off

The world is like a lucid dream: if you notice, you can affect the scene with your will. Maybe this realization will lead you to be able to manipulate the larger environment.

Which is why you become less depressed when involved in political organizing.

You dream you go upstate for a music festival, and there are floats, and you're with an ex and Laraaji is there, and Terry Riley, and the two of you are telling them things and talking about yourselves.

You talk to a man; you talk about his true crimes podcast—one of the big ones, it's his living—and death and how many people die in state parks and how you are afraid to hike alone, and he confirms that you should be afraid to hike alone.

In real life, you rub your clit with a rapidly vibrating Hitachi and find that you feel nothing. It's unclear if the Hitachi is slowly dying and so is vibrating at a different frequency, one you're not used to and that you maybe just don't like at all, or if your sex drive has vanished. You picture your favorite scenes with a smattering of favorite people: someone's legs shaking, your head between them, someone instructing you to take his glasses off, someone grabbing you and pulling you down to rub your sweat on his body, for instance —but the scenes feel empty, they don't do anything; it's as though you're an eleven-year old child trying to play with Barbies and suddenly playing pretend seems to be filled with nothing. It's just going through the motions.

Like with a depressed lover: you do all the same things, but, depending on the exact way they are depressed, maybe suddenly there is, for them and then later for you, no pull, no tension, your dick thrusts into nothing and their body is an empty sky.

The point of reading is asynchronous intimacy, and hopefully it works forever.

It seems if when we're doing research or writing, or doing any work at all, we are perhaps doing it for the current rich, who will survive into the future, past a sort of mass die-off that then allows for the planet to restore itself to equilibrium. Which seems sad—to keep building this world only for the rich, who will emerge from their bunkers and experience joy once again, while the rest of us come back as the metal rods that hold products, in, say, a CVS, or not at all.

If you're in an archive, you usually come away with a sense of apartness and difference—you can immerse yourself in these papers, which might crumple in your hands and mingle with microscopic particles of your dry skin, but you can't put yourself there. Narrative does the opposite though —you feel intimate no whispers in your ear, less a lover and more the voice in your head, like fucking your own future self.

There is beauty in life that we can't see anymore because of our minds, says a man on upstate tinder, when I'm upstate to "get away from it all."

No one would say that in NYC.

About eight years ago or so I got my then-boyfriend a picture of that Carl Sagan plaque that went into space—the one that's a sort of message in a bottle to aliens: a man's body, a woman's body, some pleasing shapes indicating perspective in the universe.

The governing trope of textual narrative is that you're in someone's head; film is incapable of duplicating this effect, in adaptations or otherwise.

Texting too has asynchronous intimacy, but my real question is how I can get myself back into the 90s and onto *Unsolved Mysteries*.

Someone sends me a picture of his dick and says he's been masturbating four times a day for the endorphin rush because he's depressed.

I once had a housemate who kept a book around called *Wiccapedia* —Wicca, not Wiki—a poppy new age book. The book suggested you can cast spells by texting things to people. Text magic.

I drive from Hudson to Kaaterskill Falls; I hike the trails and find the spot where I fell when I was here last year—I was trying to scramble up a small rock face and didn't make a step I thought I could make; I gasped and caught myself; I yelled to Lenora, who was calling my name—probably just a few yards away from me, but it was hard to hear her because of the sound of the branches and leaves rushing around in the rainy wind.

I find this spot, the spot where I fell, and am deliberately more cavalier with my scrambling. If I see a step and think I might be able to make it, I go for it. Nothing really happens. I make it up the scramble. I sit on the ground with two more rock faces in front of me and a steep decline on the other side off the trail and use the pocketknife from REI to nick the fleshy part of my knee. I pull up the picture of the dick on my phone and get a camping spoon from my backpack and dig a hole. I put the dick in the hole. I wipe some blood onto the screen. I replace the dirt. A lot of men have murdered women in state parks; this is clear from *Unsolved Mysteries*. Come for me.

Let's Pretend Today Is Not Sunday, But a Weekday

I bleed all over someone's bed and my phone knows it, advertising menstrual products to me a few hours later.

So that I guess I have a record, someone else's more accurate record.

You cum; the person fucking you wants a small break; the condom comes out covered in goopy blood and you notice then the blood near the pillow, and twice in the middle of the mattress, and once at the bottom of the mattress. And later, after you've put on underwear and laid there for a bit and talked about your workout routines and also the way that anxiousness permeates literally everything but sex, for both of you, and then given a blowjob, eventually you get up and go to the bathroom and notice another goopy strand of blood hanging out of you, which momentarily drops from your body.

Your blood will be recorded in the "oh, whoa you're bleeding a lot" and apologies in relation to the comforter—so that the waste your body's expelled might go variously to the dry cleaners and down the toilet, but has also been productive, creating money for Instagram.

So my goopy blood has produced an economic reaction, and

after we separate the bodies of the ruling class from their heads,

we'll be able to reverse the code and resuscitate all of it:

where an ad for Kotex is recorded in the book of history we'll instead get a glob of blood smeared across the page,

there to be licked up and tongued back into the body and

then into the mind and its experiences. We can dwell in it if we want: don't go to work, stay here and fuck and be fucked, like the scene in Eisenstein's *Stachka* when the factory workers have struck and a couple lays around in bed with a great fur blanket. Mid-day fucking, the opposite of work.

Except who knows: maybe instead of revolutionary bloodshed, we'll get the slow deaths of our children's children. Except we don't want children; we want periods, recorded in the ledger of history via targeted advertisements. And in our imaginations our periods signify little executions of the wealthy in our bodies, but in the daylight we don't even need a shower, usually you'd just check your makeup and leave.

**Trying to Move More Quickly Through a Wet Seal
You'd Almost Forgotten About**

I take a berry from a buckthorn—

I eat wheatgrass wrapped in wool—

Okay, sure.

And there is nothing left of my stain upon the wet earth.

There is no Hollywood story left.

If you're going to channel something
in your acupuncture dreams of an easy existence,
this ghost can talk to you.

Nobody dreamt of me.

Nobody would look me in the eye,

me being mostly grass and knees,

knees where they meet the grass
when falling and landing. Crashing

with the body, I guess;

we could think of ourselves as magazine

racks in a CVS, re-manifested into dullness

looking out the CVS window at the

sky. We're animating something that
does not need to be animated.

In the new day I sit at the bar making
typos on my phone, *I want to see you*, I type.
Dreaming of penetration, a penetration
where you're not a metal magazine rack

but a mucus membrane pried open.

I want to see you, I type, my eye the eye
of the cursor, pulsing.

Remembering being stuck inside a screendoor
on an early fall day; wouldn't you like
to be able to turn the latch,

wouldn't you like to figure it out and live again.

I want to see you, I type, and jam my finger in the hole.

The Bachelor Inseminator

In the 1985 documentary *God's Country*, which is about a rural Minnesota farming town in 1979 and in 1985, we meet a bachelor who inseminates cows for a living.

The bachelor inseminator gives his name as Steve; we don't know his last name. He participates in the community theater, where he plays a king of corn.

We see him as the King of Corn, bantering with a Queen of Corn. Wearing a crown. And then we see him at work, inseminating a cow. He explains what he is doing as he does it. He puts one plastic-covered hand into the cow's anus and uses that hand to help guide a wand that he inserts just below, into the cow's vagina. He guides the wand with the arm that is in the anus up toward the uterus, and then into each horn of the uterus, where he deposits a bull's semen.

When we meet him again in 1985, he says that he has done this to about 65,000 cows. The filmmaker asks him if he remembers the cows, if he relates to them, and he says that he remembers the owners.

Steve is in his early 30s and single, one of the town's most eligible bachelors, says the filmmaker. I assume maybe gay. Camping it up as the King of Corn in the community theater, then displacing his virility into the insem- ination of cows using a wand.

I doubt that there is a way to look up on the internet where Steve is now. He was 35 in 1985; I was 3 in 1985. Him being 32 years older than me, he's now got to be 68 or so. He's just a bit older than my parents; while he was inseminating cows, my dad was quitting his job landscaping and getting a job at the post office— more stable—so they could have me—and my mother was a quit- ting her job as a secretary at an upscale moving company so that she could stay home with me. I was fixing to enter the scene, preparing to break a crayon in half, to cry about it, to fix it with Scotch tape, to cry about the tape being on the crayon. I was steeling myself for the world's treatment, preparing to sit in a sandbox shaped like a turtle and imagine things.

Perhaps we don't live first as we exit our mothers' wombs but instead in the horns of the uteruses of cows, our spirits nesting alongside cow embryos, the spirits of the calves resting elsewhere alongside a different set of human embryos. The spirit predates the embryo and the embryo takes this spirit on when it flees the host's body. Or perhaps we return to the theory of the homunculi. Steve, the most eligible bachelor in Glencoe, uses the wand to deposit thousands of little cattle into the horns of the cow's uteruses.

Another resident in the town confirms that it would be hard to be gay there: "you'd have to have your private life in Minneapolis or somewhere else." In 1985, the filmmaker asks Steve if he has gotten married, like he said he might, and Steve says the plan had been pushed from 35 to 40 and he would make a decision by then. But also that the right person just hadn't come along yet. It occurs to me now that all the most eligible bachelors through most of history must have been queer. In 1985, my brother was about to be born; I was taught how to stand on a small stool to reach the phone and dial 911 if there were an emergency while my mother was pregnant; the prospect empowered me.

If Steve is 68 and I am 36 I wonder where he is. If he stayed in Glencoe; if he is still inseminating cows; what form my body would need to take for him to feel attraction to me and how I might create a situation in which I could fuck him. If I could make myself older, perhaps more masculine or perhaps just as I am, or perhaps younger, perhaps less cellulite, perhaps more cellulite—perhaps whatever is in his porn but really perhaps whatever would make him most comfortable—I could take this form and let him lube up his fingers, I could remove my harness—constructed out of the skin of a dead cow—and he could let the harness rest on his hands as he plied me with the silicone dick, me on my knees and running my fingers inside my body, him behind handling the dildo, my fingers not at all like wands; I pull my fingers out after I cum and shove them into his mouth. When he cums it's onto the bedding; we don't wipe it up but let it sit there and hope it soaks through to the mattress. He watches it dry up. We leave the room. We walk out. Reagan is president; I'm seventy years old; I can't feel my face.

Ars Poetica

Maybe poems have always been about remembering and for some reason I was fighting it. Like I didn't want to care about remembering things. I mean no one wants to read something about how one person's life is so precious, but I do think I thought poems could be about the world and therefore not about me. And, you know, I still want that—more the world, less me, but also kind of all of me here, to haunt you and live in this book after I die. Roaming the earth and getting pulped and roaming some more.

David Berman, one of the first poets I loved, died last week and I keep reading "Self-Portrait at 28" over and over again. I wish I could write this poem as a David Berman rip-off but I can't get in the mode. I can only note that I first read that poem when I was 21 and now I'm so much older; now I'm 37 and to think the words "Self-Portrait at 28" is something different than what it once was. I didn't read that poem when I was 28, but I'm certain there was a moment when we all re-enacted the ending. When my voice was what filled my cat's thoughts, as Berman's speaker's voice fills his dog's thoughts in the poem:

> You see,
> his mind can only hold one thought at a time
> and when he looks up and cocks his head.
> For a single moment
> my voice is everything:

Self-portrait at 28.

The trick is that we get David Berman's portrait through himself seeing his dog seeing him and telling it to us. For a single moment. There are some things poetry is ill-suited for, but it's extremely good at describing the single moment. I guess that poetry can't help but be precious then, and also that it's always a metonym: let's get at this moment and use it as a thumbnail for all the other moments.

The first lines of that poem are "I know it's a bad title / but I'm giving it to myself as a gift."

I remember first hearing the term "Ars Poetica" in poetry class, College of Charleston, circa 2002, and thinking that ars poeticas seemed like the worst because they suggested there was nothing to write about: if we're making poems about poems instead of about the world, and the world isn't worthy of note, and there's no experience of a thing to point to, then why stay alive?

Whereas now I'd like art to consume as much of life as possible; if art is the katamari ball and life is all the objects in the world, the objects that have not yet been subsumed into the katamari ball are always too many and make me anxious.

Writing about memory instead of about the world makes me scared —who will read this poem, I think, I mean, who are the people I don't think of as the readers for it but who might nonetheless see it?

But I'm going to write this here—let's make it performative, a speech act:

> *If you're reading this and I should forgive something you've done, I forgive it. If you're reading this and I should ask your forgiveness, I'm asking it.*

I take a walk with a lover. We get bagels; we take them to Grand Army Plaza; we sit on a bench; I don't spill anything on myself. He tells me about Mormonism and I have nothing to offer since he knows everything about Catholicism. I say that maybe we're missing something with confession. Now people go to therapy, but therapy doesn't involve speech acts: my therapist can help me, but she can't forgive me. Forgiveness is pretty social.

I mean: sin exists. There is that Flannery O'Connor story in which a very young boy has barely left his house, and his grandfather, who is his caregiver, has also has barely left the house. The grandfather has been to Atlanta once and is afraid of it; they're in rural Georgia; the grandfather agrees to catch the train with the boy and take him to Atlanta for the day. The grandfather doesn't know how to do a lot of things outside of his normal routine; he is scared. When they're in Atlanta, very much a big frightening city, they get lost. The young boy accidentally knocks someone over, if I'm remembering it correctly, and suddenly people are yelling at him, demanding he pay money, threatening to throw him in jail, etc. The boy is terrified. The grandfather, who had been distracted by something else and so had been walking a bit behind, sees this happening and pretends he doesn't know the boy, even when the boy points at him and appeals to him. The grandfather, who does not have any money, walks away, leaving the boy alone with people yelling at him that he must pay. The grandfather eventually finds the boy again—he feels regret after—but that doesn't change it, and O'Connor is so dark and brutal and good. It's like she's taunting us, daring us into Catholicism—*you think sin doesn't exist? Let me think of something horrific; there is no way this isn't sin.* And we nod in horror.

Men leave their wives for younger women all the time, sometimes leaving their kids as well. Even in commie circles. And every time I definitely think this is a sin.

When I left a partner, my first therapist afterward asked me if I missed my partner and when I said yes, she said, "well, he bore witness to your existence for five years," which was true. But she also said that as though it were explanatory.

The next time I fall in love, the person I'm in love with will never remember how the cats used to crawl into a hole in the box spring of our old bed, for instance, and sleep in the box spring so that if you couldn't find them, you'd eventually look under the bed for two weighty pockets of fabric hanging down lower than the rest,

and you'd poke the fabric and find their soft heavy bodies and
they'd mew and stir as you woke them.

And when I go out now with people my own age, I think wow,
you've lived a whole life already; it's not like you're ever going to
be able to explain it all to me. James Baldwin just kills off Rufus,
the character the narrative has thus far followed, a third of the
way through *Another Country*. Which is a weird brutal move you
can't do in poetry either—you have to have narrative to build the
protagonist. In poetry we're ready for one moment to be special
and unlike the next. In fiction we want to believe the continuity
of the narrative—that's the premise for narrative working—but it
doesn't occur to us that the narrative can still continue without the
protagonist. I.e., there is a social world. For a single moment your
voice is everything to someone somewhere—but that's why it's just
a single moment.

I'm eating my bagel at Grand Army Plaza. There should be more
of a concept of sin in the world, we say; we should just get what
sin is right. When do you reach the age of accountability in Mormon
theology? Eight. When do you reach it in Catholic theology? Seven.
My lover is nine years younger than me so I've had ten years' more
sinning than he has, in total.

Part of me doesn't doubt that the sins last longer than the rest of
it: if, for instance, Flannery O'Connor created a story about a
grandfather who sinned by forsaking his grandson, that grand-
father's sin lives longer and wider than, say, the tumbling buffalo
that David Wojnarowicz dreams, since the tumbling buffalo involves
no sin, and since, because it involves no sin, in or out of the frame
of the dream, we want to hold it in our brains as long as we can—
look, this buffalo has survived since the 80s, penetrated out of its
dream world and off of Wojnarowicz's lips and onto a tape diary
and from the tape diary into a paperback book printed in many
thousands of copies and from that book into my brain and from
my brain into this poem, to do battle with the awful grandfather

in the Flannery O'Connor story, but, god, all you feel when you read the O'Connor story is a pit of sickness in your stomach. What if you woke up so guilty; what if you've been so guilty and it wasn't justified and the shame of it just hung there.

What if sin is less ephemeral than all the rest of it? I guess that must be how someone came up with the concept of Hell, which certainly must have predated Heaven.

I tell my lover that I want him to make me Mormon, and he replies that he never got to the level at which you can do that, but his brothers did.

Anything that made me Mormon would also just be a speech act. Speech act upon speech act, all to apologize.

I watch *Fleabag*, a show about guilt, and I cry more than other people seem to have cried when watching it. Also: the hot priest, the confessional —I feel like Twitter missed that what's actually hot about the hot priest is the promise of forgiveness.

The metaphor is that sexuality holds out a promise of forgiveness, or of not in fact needing it—I'm supposed to need forgiveness for this sex sin, but since the rubric that dictates that is bullshit, in fact perhaps I don't need forgiveness at all—and what calls the question is when our main character pursues the hot priest, someone who can forgive with a speech act, and winds up on her knees in a confessional booth.

And the promise of forgiveness is, perhaps, the promise of being able to love your lover rather than fucking and simultaneously spiking the camera —that is, turning to it and looking at the viewer, when previously you have not looked at the viewer—to comment on the fucking, a move that's better than some moves and worse than others and that felt overly familiar to me as I watched the show.

Fleabag takes the camera spike trope from *The Office* and subsequently so many other shows—main characters turn to face the camera and address the camera cleverly and sarcastically to comment on the antics of everyone around them, of the world they're living in—and show it for what it is. Spiking the camera is about depression. Maybe in the British office the depressive camera spike is a welcome critique of office culture: our straight man looks to us, the viewers (framed as a documentary crew), instead of those around him—don't we all feel like this in the office, wouldn't we all like someone who is not crazy to talk to, someone to share a glance with? Maybe in the American office, more depressingly, it's a very un-self-conscious sort of generalized depression—humor equals a constant light mockery and distance from one's surroundings; it's almost like that bit in Mark Fisher, where we're all imagining a Big Other—we think someone likes things as they are, when in fact no one does, but we constantly project onto our environment some sort of culture that everyone consents to and likes except for ourselves. Derisiveness is the only mode we can operate in, and so we get Steven Colbert and every other wry news show that is like it, too, where the world is the office. We're all being winked at by the smartest person on the sitcom, and we get him, and he gets us, and everyone else doesn't get it. Something about it feels very late nineties / aughts / pre-Occupy, when, finally, like Fisher predicted, a sort of veil lifted in political life and many of us saw each other there, hating the same things, and stopped looking only to the imagined viewer.

But *Fleabag* is different from *The Office*. It posits spiking the camera not as a clever default from a witty protagonist, but as a depressive symptom. Being too clever for everything around you, wanting to have a nonexistent viewer who looks at the world and helps you disengage from it through your shared cleverness. Which makes clear, maybe, that people liking the American version of *The Office* is pathological, and that instead you should watch *Fleabag* and weep for hours.

It's the priest, the priest who's both a real human and a person you want to fuck and also someone with the power to forgive, who can see that you're doing something weird by addressing the camera, and can, with a lot of effort on your own part, get you to push the camera away, and eventually say goodbye to it, and then, from there, behave as if you're in a non-self-conscious piece of art, a piece of art that isn't meta, i.e., so that you aren't even in art, you're just in the world. The show ends.

I feel jealous that the screen can break it down like that, since poetry doesn't work that way and instead all we can do here is address the audience.

When I was jogging upstate, listening to Judee Sill and looking over the Hudson at the Catskill Mountains at sunset, at the rays of light peering through the clouds up by the mountaintops, it occurred to me that maybe all of religion, or at least Judeo-Christian religion, is a really elaborate metaphor about mountains and perspective. Which seemed embarrassingly silly—like, really, all this because people were like whoa, mountains, I can see so much from up here! Someone must be up even higher! And when I'm in the valley, light comes through seemingly in proximity to the mountains! Galaxy brain. God is who can see it all at once.

It's the notion that, for better or worse, someone has a ledger. That things aren't in fact, moment by moment, and continually washed away, that instead everyone is held to account and somewhere we'll be happy on account of the good things we did earlier, and elsewhere Jeff Bezos, say, and his peers will have their blood spilt eternally. Even if all of this happens only in some abstract way, just from someone looking down from just above the summit of a mountain for a very long time.

Which I guess would be some comfort. Someone, I guess, would watch the dog in David Berman's poem, watch him hear the speaker call him. But it already doesn't work: if God is about mountain tops,

God still doesn't have access to the full range of sensory and psychic experiences of the world.

Maybe someone watches us with the ledger, but the ledger doesn't record much. Instead you've got to write the poem. David Berman writes the poem about the dog running in a field and hearing his name: for a single moment / my voice is everything / self-portrait at 28. But the dog calls back, spiking the camera, if David Berman is the camera man and I am putting myself in David Berman's shoes. You fill the dog's head and the dog fills yours. The reader overhears it. God looks down from a mountaintop and likes what he sees, his vision obscured by nothing but the dog's furry head and your head, also furry.

Let's Say It's Possible After All

I'm watching an episode of *Unsolved Mysteries* about Stonehenge and wheat fields.

But last night I went to a hexing of Brett Kavanaugh. Not to hex but to help escort people to the train safely, since the Proud Boys had threatened to show up at the hexing and, presumably, beat people up.

During the last twelve years, says Robert Stack in the late 1980s, more than 750 large, perfectly symmetrical circles have formed overnight in seemingly random fields of corn, wheat, and other crops.

The question no one can answer is, how did the circles get there?

We had received a text message before the hexing telling us that InfoWars was there, so many of us had covered our faces. You could tell the anarchist and anarchist-adjacent left by their bandanas, but you could not tell much else: there were Christian protesters and potential alt-right people and a larger swath of lefties and a lot of witches and some lefty punks and some lefty sort of metal guys and some right-wingers dressed like frat guys and some right-wingers dressed like punks, maybe—though hard to say—and some Christians dressed like hippies, it seemed.

And so it was, at least at the beginning, difficult to tell who was who, which is rare for New York. For instance the owner of the occult bookstore was wearing a sort of dapper suit and carrying a cane. For a moment, before someone told me who he was, I thought he might be an alt-right figure, with the cane as a sort of potential weapon.

In the late 80s, farmers described crop circles with notes of awe in their voices.

"One was a beautiful quintuplet set: a large circle with four smaller ones around it.

They have a neat, perfect pattern, from a center, where it's flattened."

The Proud Boys did not show up to the hexing after all. Everyone smoked cigarettes and occasionally taunted the evangelicals, but in a sort of jokey way; they seemed relatively harmless compared to the Proud Boys.

At one point I saw someone I'd been on a date with and waved at her; she didn't seem to recognize me. Were you wearing your mask, asked Lenora later when I told her this, and I had been.

And a huge circle had appeared in the wheat.

It was so perfect, really.

The question no one can answer is, how did the circles get there?

I've been here since October 1957, someone says. And he describes the circles, from year to year.

"They have a neat, perfect pattern, from a center, where it's flattened."

"The most wonderful thing about it is when you actually go out the night before to look for a circle and there's nothing there, it's just a lovely field of growing corn and then the following morning, when you get up early in the morning in the first light of day and suddenly there is the circle, you just can't believe it."

Some circles have satellites; others have rings. But some have both satellites and rings.

And in one theory, the circles are created by hundreds of hedge-hogs running in unison.

And in another theory, the creator of the circles cupped my breast in their hand while the hexing occurred.

And in yet a third theory, I chewed the inside of my mouth, anxiously, and the field that is my mouth correlates to another year and a larger space, and the circle appears; my chewing has activated the hedgehogs to run.

And I feel fear and also exhilaration; the threat of our bodies has stopped the Proud Boys from appearing, a sort of hex whether the hex works or not. And I let the hedgehogs in miniature run around my mouth, feeling their snouts brush my gums and their paws pattering along my walls, and Gavin McInnes stands in a crop circle in progress. It is so awkward when three people try to make out at once, but we lift our bandanas and we do; in this world we're a comical thruple in anarchist gear, but in that other a giant tongue lobs a body across a field and it dies from the impact.

Oh

I rewatch *God's Country* again.

It's not just the bachelor inseminator: I would also like to sleep with the pig farmer, the pig farmer who likes to work for himself. In real life I sleep with a man who tells me about his failed attempt to be an entrepreneur, something he tried because he wanted to work for himself. It humbled him, he said.

I'd like to sleep with the pig farmer in his youth, at the time of the documentary; I'd need a time travel machine to do it, and I wonder if it is even possible to find a contemporary pig farmer working under similar conditions.

The contemporary pig farmer's life would be different; I speculate he'd be less happy and that pig farming has gotten harder.

It is probably impossible to sleep with anyone right now who has a hopeful view of the future and is not an idiot. I mean: in 1985 I bet you could sleep with many people, most people even, and the person you chose as your lover would think the world was going to keep getting better and better.

I'll probably never fuck someone who imagines there might be benevolent aliens in space.

Or that the situation is infinite.

Or that we are small in comparison to a vastness.

Instead I'll fuck only people aware of impending doom.

One lover likes my sweat, and I have been self-conscious of my sweat for as long as I remember. I am on top of him; he is rubbing my clit while I fuck him; I feel sweat bead on my forehead and watch it splash on his chest; he sees me notice this and begin to wipe away my sweat and says no no, put it on me, put it on me and pulls me down to rub my torso against his; our bodies are very slick.

And this is hot because sweat is hot, but it is also hot because he has changed my shame to pride via his direction.

This is no way to end this poem, which I had intended to be about space exploration.

And socialism.

And how people once thought that better forms of civilization existed elsewhere.

And that our world too could be better.

And how the passage of time means that I'll never fuck someone with the structures of thought that people had in the 70s or 80s, at least not in their youth.

It's a good sort of water-into-wine trick to be able to make something one had felt was unattractive attractive, and of course very useful as a corrective in the case that a lover keeps apologizing for their sweat, for instance, something so goofy that even I have always known not to do it, even before I was taught to like my sweat.

However, if I were going to be very convincingly told I'm wrong about something and have my view of it radically changed through pleasure, I'd rather that thing be my notion that there is very little hope. This task seems like one for someone from *God's Country*, from the first part of the movie, which was filmed in 1979, and not from the second part, which was filmed in 1985 and chronicles how much bleaker things have gotten by the time the filmmaker returns to finish his movie.

I'm on vacation upstate, lying in bed in an AirBnB that has floor to ceiling windows covered with a sheer curtain. That is, anyone could be watching me.

I would like the 1979 pig farmer to breech my screen and step out of it, as though he were the Kool-Aid man from the same period, a giant anthropomorphic pitcher of Kool-Aid bursting through, pigs galloping behind him. "Oh yeah" is a perfectly respectable thing to say during sex; this would be all he'd need to say; he'd pour the Kool-Aid on me; it would look like blood; it'd be a single act of pouring and then I would crawl into his empty glass body and curl up in it, dreaming of what comes next.